Flossmoor Public Library
1000 Sterling Avenue
Flossmoor, IL 60422-1295
Phone: (708) 798-3600

1ST
IN FASHION
× × × × ×

SAM FOSTER
SUNGLASSES SUCCESS

REBECCA FELIX

Checkerboard Library

An Imprint of Abdo Publishing
abdopublishing.com

ABDOPUBLISHING.COM

Published by Abdo Publishing, a division of ABDO, PO Box 398166, Minneapolis, Minnesota 55439.
Copyright © 2018 by Abdo Consulting Group, Inc. International copyrights reserved in all countries.
No part of this book may be reproduced in any form without written permission from the publisher.
Checkerboard Library™ is a trademark and logo of Abdo Publishing.

Printed in the United States of America, North Mankato, Minnesota
062017
092017

THIS BOOK CONTAINS
RECYCLED MATERIALS

Design: Emily O'Malley, Mighty Media, Inc.
Production: Emily O'Malley, Mighty Media, Inc.
Series Editor: Katherine Hengel Frankowski
Cover Photographs: Public domain (left); Shutterstock (right)
Interior Photographs: Alamy, pp. 23, 25; AP Images, p. 27; iStockphoto pp. 5, 11 (top); Public domain, p. 15; Shutterstock, pp. 10 (top), 10 (bottom), 11 (middle), 11 (bottom), 17, 19, 21; Wikimedia Commons, pp. 7, 8, 13

Publisher's Cataloging-in-Publication Data

Names: Felix, Rebecca, author.
Title: Sam Foster: sunglasses success / by Rebecca Felix.
Other titles: Sunglasses success
Description: Minneapolis, MN : Abdo Publishing, 2018. | Series: First in fashion |
    Includes bibliographical references and index.
Identifiers: LCCN 2016962473 | ISBN 9781532110740 (lib. bdg.) |
    ISBN 9781680788594 (ebook)
Subjects: LCSH: Foster, Sam,--Juvenile literature. | Fashion designer--
    United States--Biography--Juvenile literature. | Inventor--United States--
    Biography--Juvenile literature. | Sunglasses--Juvenile literature.
Classification: DDC 391 [B]--dc23
LC record available at http://lccn.loc.gov/2016962473

CONTENTS

MADE IN THE SHADE

It is a superbright, sunny day. You step outside and immediately **squint**. You slide on some sunglasses and smile. Now you can see without squinting. And, you look pretty cool too!

You can thank Sam Foster for your fashionable, useful eyewear. He was the first to **mass-produce** modern sunglasses. In 1929, Foster began selling the product along the beaches of Atlantic City, New Jersey. He sold his plastic sunglasses to shoppers and beachgoers. The dark lenses made it easier to see in bright daylight. They also protected the wearer's eyes from harmful sun rays.

Foster's sunglasses soon rose in popularity with help from celebrities. Before long, sunglasses became more than protective gear. They became stylish **accessories**. Soon, kids and adults around the world were wearing sunglasses.

Sunglasses are a great way for you and your friends to show off your personalities!

STONE & BONE

Sunglasses have been around for a long time. **Inuit** tribes used sunglasses more than 800 years ago. The Arctic regions Inuit people lived in were very snowy and bright. To protect their eyes, Inuit people crafted sunglasses out of walrus bones and **caribou** antlers.

Other **cultures** also made sunglasses. In ancient China, some judges wore frames made of stone. These frames were fitted with lenses made of smoky **quartz**. The glasses' purpose was not to protect the judges' eyes from sun. Instead, the stones hid their eyes from others! It was harder for people to guess what the judges were thinking.

SUNGLASSES AS SHIELDS

Many people wear sunglasses to conceal things. For example, people with eye deformities often wear sunglasses. Celebrities may wear shades to try to hide their faces. Sunglasses can also hide emotions.

Inuit sunglasses fit tightly on the wearer's face, so light could only enter through the slits.

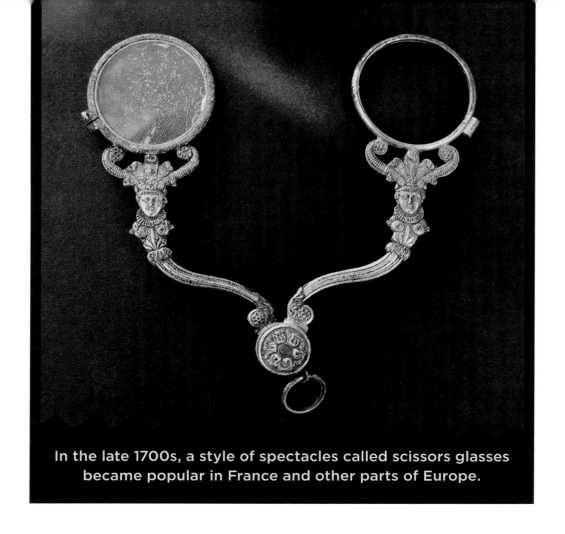

In the late 1700s, a style of spectacles called scissors glasses became popular in France and other parts of Europe.

TINTS, TREATMENTS & TRENDS

The first lens to correct vision was created in Italy in the 1200s. This lens was made from a type of **quartz** called beryl. The beryl was ground into a curved shape.

The stone became a magnifying glass! It made objects appear larger and more focused. Many people wanted these new corrective lenses. Glass was easier to obtain than beryl. So most lens makers began crafting lenses out of glass.

In the 1700s, English inventor James Ayscough developed the first tinted glass lenses. He added a blue or green color to lenses. This made it easier to look at bright objects, such as white paper. Ayscough also introduced a new type of frame. It had hinged side pieces that rested on the ears.

In the 1800s, lenses were tinted yellow and brown. These tint colors helped block light. Protection from light became a key feature in eyewear. In the early 1900s, an inventor sold such eyewear in a beachside shop. His sunglasses would launch an unstoppable fashion trend.

FASHION
TIME MACHINE

AVIATORS, 1940s During **World War II**, the United States Army Air Corps created special sunglasses for its pilots. The glasses had large, teardrop-shaped lenses. This shape protected the pilot's entire eye from the sun. Civilians soon adopted the new style!

WAYFARERS, 1950s In the 1950s, the eyewear company Ray-Ban created Wayfarer sunglasses. They had thick, plastic frames. At that time, most frames were made of metal. Ray-Ban's frames also came in new, bright colors.

OVERSIZED, 1970s Former First Lady Jacqueline Kennedy Onassis was a fashion icon. In the 1970s, a photo of her in sunglasses was published. The glasses had black frames and huge, round lenses. Oversized shades became instantly popular!

WRAPAROUNDS, 1990s Wraparound sunglasses have wide lenses and tight-fitting frames. They stay put on a wearer's face. Wraparound sunglasses became popular with athletes in the 1990s. Soon, they were popular with sports fans, celebrities, and everyone in between!

SHUTTER SHADES, 2000s In 2006, rapper Kanye West wore a pair of **custom** shades on stage. They didn't have solid lenses. Instead, they had **horizontal** plastic bars that connected to the frames. These horizontal pieces looked like window shutters. The trend soon took off around the United States!

PLASTICS PIONEER

Sam Foster was born in 1883 and grew up in Austria. He had four sisters and two brothers. In 1897, his family **immigrated** to the United States. They settled in Massachusetts.

As a teenager, Foster worked instead of attending high school. He sold fireworks, worked as a waiter, and made jewelry. He later met and married a woman named Jennie. In 1907, they had a son named Joseph. That same year, Foster started a new career. He took a job making plastic combs at Viscoloid Company in Leominster, Massachusetts.

In 1914, a fashion trend led to near **disaster** for Foster and Viscoloid Company. Movie star Irene Castle cut off her long hair! Her fans across

FASHION FACTOID

In the early 1900s, there were more than 24 comb factories in Leominster. The city was nicknamed "Comb City."

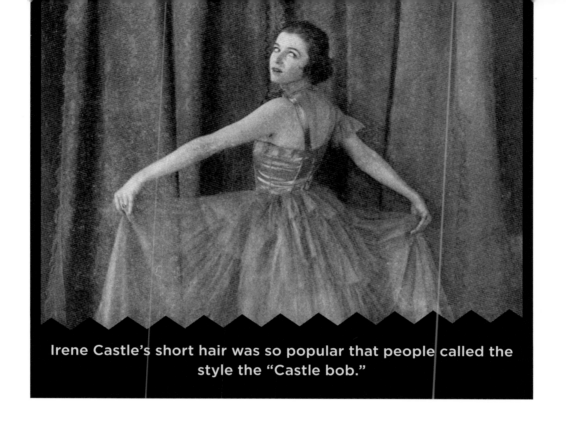

Irene Castle's short hair was so popular that people called the style the "Castle bob."

the country did too. This new, short style was easy to maintain without combs. Almost immediately, comb sales dropped.

Plastics factories had to adapt. The Viscoloid Company found ways to produce and sell other plastic products. These included jewelry, small toys, and dice. This new manufacturing know-how would serve Foster well in the years ahead.

CREATING A COMPANY

Foster worked for Viscoloid Company until 1919. Then, he decided to open his own plastics plant. He called his business the Foster Manufacturing Company.

Foster soon hired a salesperson named William Grant. Eventually, Foster made Grant a partner in his business. Foster paid to legally change the company name to Foster Grant Company.

However, several months later, Grant left the company. Foster did not want to spend more money on name changes. So, he kept the name Foster Grant.

During its first year, Foster Grant made plastic jewelry and hair **accessories**. In 1920, it received several big orders from Goody Hair Products. Goody was a large hair accessory company. The owners of Goody knew it took skill to make small, detailed plastic pieces. So,

SUPER CELLULOID

Celluloid was the first **synthetic** plastic. It was created in the 1860s. Celluloid is stiff and tough, yet also **flexible**. It softens when heated. When soft, it can be shaped and pressed into molds. Once the plastic cools, it hardens.

Sam Foster

Goody hired Foster to produce plastic dice too. Soon,
Foster Grant's business was booming. Competing plastics
companies took notice!

15

NEW VISION

In 1924, the Foster Grant company was growing. It needed more space. So, Foster moved his company to a larger building in Leominster.

More space allowed Foster to expand his product line. He started making tiny birdcages that held plastic birds. He also made plastic crayons that wrote on special notepads. Then, in the 1920s, Foster began producing plastic glasses with tinted lenses.

Foster's first sunglasses were sold as children's toys. They cost just 10 cents a pair. Then, in 1929, Foster created an adult version of the glasses. He called them Foster Grants. Now, all he needed were customers. He decided to travel to Atlantic City, New Jersey.

At the time, Atlantic City was a busy tourist town. Many people visited its beaches. There were many shops along the beaches' **boardwalks**. Foster made a deal

Atlantic City is a famous tourist destination. The city's boardwalk is known for its shops and its amusement park, Steel Pier.

with a **boardwalk** store called Woolworth's. Woolworth's began selling Foster's glasses to beachgoers for 10 cents a pair. Sales were slow at first, but they wouldn't be for long.

SEEING STARS

Movie stars helped give Foster's products a big boost. In the 1920s and 1930s, American **cinema** was on the rise. As movies gained popularity, so did the actors in them. Actors were seen as fashion icons. And, many movie stars wore sunglasses!

Actors in Hollywood, California, wore sunglasses throughout the 1920s. The dark lenses protected their eyes from the bright film lights. Off the set, sunglasses offered protection from the bright California sun. Sunglasses also offered actors privacy from photographers.

The more famous actors became, the more their photos were published. Photos of movie stars wearing

CELEBRITIES & SHADES

Celebrities have always created sunglasses trends. In the 1950s, actor Marilyn Monroe made cat-eye sunglasses popular. In the 1970s, singer Elton John kept the oversized sunglasses trend alive. Pop star Britney Spears wore tiny, wire-framed shades in the 1990s. So did twin actors Mary-Kate and Ashley Olsen. Soon, young girls around the nation were following suit.

In the 2010s, celebrities, including pop star Gwen Stefani, brought back the cat-eye sunglasses style from the 1950s.

sunglasses were all over the **media**. Sunglasses became associated with glamour and style. Soon, many people wanted a pair of sunglasses!

MOLDING SUCCESS

As the fame of film stars rose, so did the demand for sunglasses. Foster Grant was producing sunglasses as fast as it could. Still, it was falling short of demand. Luckily, in 1931, a new **technology** made Foster's business much more **efficient**.

Foster learned that European plastics manufacturers were using a new technology. It was called **injection molding**. Injection molding allowed manufacturers to create detailed products much more quickly.

The usual process for creating plastic products was messy and difficult. Workers melted small plastic pieces into liquid. Then they poured the hot liquid into molds. Everything had to be done quickly, before the liquid hardened.

Injection molding machines were different. They were **automated** and regulated temperatures. Foster bought

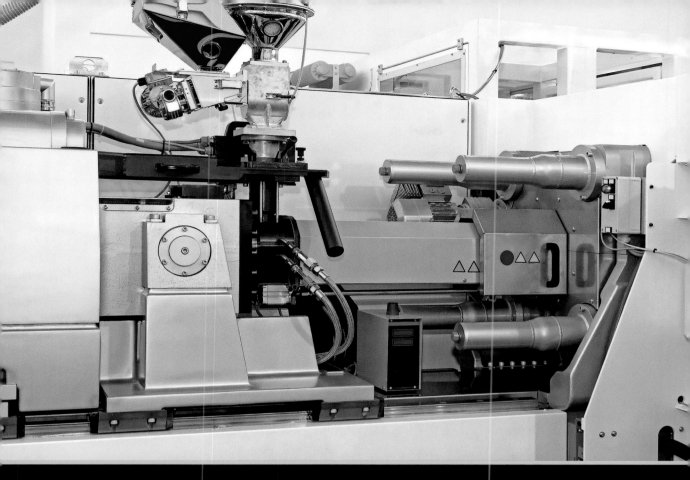

Injection molding machines are used to create goods made from plastic, metal, glass, and more.

three **injection molding** machines for Foster Grant. Soon, Foster's new machines were up and running. And, he was able to produce sunglasses more **efficiently**.

AWESOME ADS

With its new machines, Foster Grant made sunglasses at an incredible rate. By the 1940s, Foster Grant was selling its shades overseas. Then, in 1942, Foster retired. He left behind a capable team, including his son, Joseph. Foster died on February 27, 1966, at age 82.

Meanwhile, in the 1960s, Foster Grant's new leaders hired an advertising agency. Together, they developed an ad campaign. The campaign focused on sunglasses' popularity with film stars. It played up how cool and mysterious celebrities were.

The agency created print ads of famous actors wearing Foster Grants. The ads' **slogan** was, "Who's Behind Those Foster Grants?" The ad campaign was a hit! Foster Grants became more popular than ever.

FASHION FACTOID

Foster Grants were the first sunglasses to use lens coatings that blocked **ultraviolet** rays.

BUY A PAIR OF FOSTER GRANT OPTI-CLIPOVER SUNGLASSES

GET A SPARE FREE!

They're the only clip-on sunglasses with the ff77® Lens—precision made to keep your eyes safe from glare. Clip on in a second. Won't affect corrective qualities of your prescription lenses. Styles for men and women. **Get two pair—a $2.98 value—**

Eyeglass

Foster Grant offered special deals in newspaper advertisements to attract customers.

COMPANY CHANGES

Foster Grant was a well-known company throughout the 1960s. But its sales decreased in the 1970s. In 1986, the investment firm Andlinger & Co. bought the company.

Under the new owners, Foster Grant went into debt. By 1989, the company was spending more money than it was making. In 1990, Foster Grant went **bankrupt**. It was bought and sold by other companies several times in the early 1990s. Then, in 1993, new owners brought Foster Grant out of debt. It was once again one of the world's largest producers of sunglasses!

In the years ahead, Foster Grant continued to grow and change. New features, styles, and lenses were introduced. Today, Foster Grants come in many shapes. These

FASHION FACTOID

In 2017, social **media** app Snapchat released sunglasses with built-in cameras. The glasses were called Snapchat Spectacles!

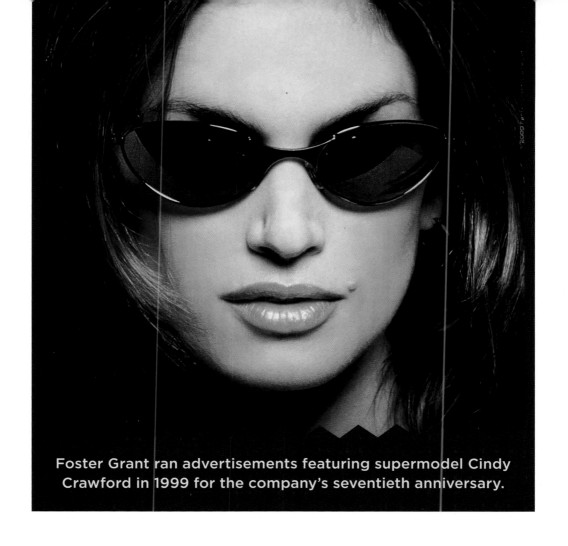

Foster Grant ran advertisements featuring supermodel Cindy Crawford in 1999 for the company's seventieth anniversary.

include square, round, and rectangle. The company offers styles for women, men, and kids. It has sunglasses designed for driving. Foster Grant even has a special sunglasses collection related to the Star Wars movies.

ICONIC ACCESSORY

Through the years, sunglasses have come in many shapes, colors, and materials. Modern frames are made of plastic and metal. Lenses are plastic, **polarized**, mirrored, and more. There are tinted lenses that clip onto regular glasses. Some companies even make superdark sunglasses that astronauts wear in space!

Sunglasses still function as protective eyewear. Most sunglasses have some sort of **ultraviolet** protection. In fact, every pair of Foster Grant lenses provides 100 percent ultraviolet protection.

SUNGLASSES SLANG

Sunglasses have many nicknames around the world. In North America, they are often called *shades*. People in India call dark sunglasses *glares*. They are known as *sunnies* in South Africa, the United Kingdom, New Zealand, and Australia. Southern Australians sometimes call them *spekkies* too. In Scotland, sunglasses are called *glecks*.

A lot has changed since Sam Foster's first pair of sunglasses. But glasses with dark lenses have remained useful and fashionable. Today, sunglasses are a part of most people's **wardrobe**. And, they have forever changed the way we see on sunny days.

In 2014, *The Vampire Diaries* actor Kat Graham became the new face behind Foster Grants. A collection was created around her personal style.

TIMELINE

1883

Sam Foster is born.

1897

The Foster family moves to the United States.

1907

Foster begins working in a plastics factory.

1919

Foster opens his own plastics business, Foster Manufacturing Company. The company name is soon changed to Foster Grant.

1929

Foster sells his first sunglasses, called Foster Grants, on the Atlantic City Boardwalk.

1920s–1930s

Celebrities embrace sunglasses, and they become a popular fashion accessory.

1942

Foster retires from Foster Grant at age 59.

1966

Foster dies on February 27.

1990

Foster Grant goes bankrupt.

1993

New owners bring Foster Grant out of debt. It regains its title as one of the top sunglasses manufacturers in the world.

GLOSSARY

accessory—an object or device that adds to the beauty, convenience, or effectiveness of something.

automate—to have mechanical or electronic devices replace human operators.

bankrupt—legally declared unable to pay something owed.

boardwalk—a walkway made of planks, usually along a beach.

caribou—a type of large deer that lives in cold, northern regions.

cinema—the art or business of making movies.

culture—the customs, arts, and tools of a nation or a people at a certain time.

custom—one of a kind, or made to order.

disaster—an event that causes damage, destruction, and often loss of life.

efficient—able to produce a desired result, especially without wasting time or energy.

flexible—able to bend easily.

horizontal—level with the horizon, or side to side.

immigrate—to enter another country to live.

injection molding—the shaping of rubber or plastic items by forcing heated material into a mold.

Inuit—a member of a group of people native to northern North America and Greenland.

mass-produce—to make in large quantities, usually using machines.

media—a form or system of communication, information, or entertainment. It includes television, radio, and newspapers.

polarized—coated with a special chemical film that helps reduce glare.

quartz—a common mineral that is often found in the form of colorless transparent crystals but is sometimes brightly colored.

slogan—a word or a phrase used to express a position, a stand, or a goal.

squint—to partly close the eyes.

synthetic—something that is human-made by a chemical process. Synthetic products include plastic and many kinds of fabrics, dyes, and drugs.

technology—the use of science for practical purposes.

ultraviolet—relating to a type of light that cannot be seen with the human eye.

wardrobe—a collection of clothing.

World War II—from 1939 to 1945, fought in Europe, Asia, and Africa. Great Britain, France, the United States, the Soviet Union, and their allies were on one side. Germany, Italy, Japan, and their allies were on the other side.

WEBSITES

To learn more about First in Fashion, visit **abdobooklinks.com**.
These links are routinely monitored and updated to provide
the most current information available.

INDEX